I PRAYED FOR MY REFRIGERATOR

AND OTHER STORES OF FAITH

CAROL L. HOWELL

There is nothing more important in life than our relationship with God. How can this relationship grow? Through constant communication with Him, we can have a deep relationship that will sustain us no matter what life situation we may experience. That is the reason for this book. It seems my life has been a case study in "odd things" for which I felt the need to drop to my knees and pray. In looking back on these things, it seemed appropriate to share these stories with others. Thus, I Prayed For My Refrigerator And Other Stories of Faith was born.

I want to thank my husband, Michael, for supporting me in my writing. He is always encouraging me to pursue what I am passionate about, and writing about My Heavenly Father is one of those things. Michael, thank you for moving a desk upstairs so I could have an office. Thank you for moving that desk downstairs and replacing it with a different desk. And, finally, thank you for moving the first desk BACK upstairs because I liked it better. You are my love and my life!

To Brandie and Mike, I hope this book will be a reminder to pray, pray, pray. This will be the basis for a wonderful   marriage! I love you, both! Thank you for giving me Baby Tessa (be still my heart!)

This book is in memory of my Momma, Vera. Momma, I might be entirely envious you are in heaven, worshipping our Lord, walking on streets of gold (you always did love jewelry), eating really good food without gaining weight, and loving every single minute of your new life. I miss you, and I will ALWAYS love you!

CONTENTS

"The value of consistent prayer is not that He will hear us, but that we will hear Him."

(WILLIAM MCGILL)

INTRODUCTION

"For we know, all things work together for good for those who love God, who are thee called according to His purpose." (Romans 8:28, King James Version)

T his verse has been my Rock for most of my life. There has not been a hardship I have encountered where this verse did not play a significant role in guiding me. I do wonder, however, why God would love me so much that He would care about ALL the details of my life. I have seen Him work in magnificent ways, and I have seen His handprint in small, seemingly insignificant ways. The truth is, anything God touches is very significant. Why, though, with all that goes on in our world, would He care about me, my life, and – dare I say- even my refrigerator?

There have been so many times I have prayed for big things, but I would like to tell you a few stories where I have seen God answer prayers regarding things you might think were unusual to pray about. I think it is entirely possible God giggles sometimes when I pray, but He is never offended at my requests. Yes, I have prayed for my refrigerator. When the refrigerator had the "flu," or something that caused it not to operate properly, praying for it just made sense to me. The last thing I wanted to do was shell out funds for a repair man. I believe God honored the fact that my husband and I are good stewards of the money He gives us. So, when I prayed and ask ed Him to please help with whatever problem we might be facing, I believe He honored that request. He hears, and He understands, any life situation we might be facing.

Why wouldn't we take our concerns to Him – even concerns that most people would not consider "normal" to pray about? The answer lies in the relationship we have with God.

Let me tell you another story. My step-dad, who stole my heart the first time I met him, was an amazing man. This wonderful man had lung cancer. He died about nine months after we got the horrible news of the disease that was ravaging his body. I watched him suffer from shoulder pain as a result of the cancer, and I stayed close by as he experienced the side effects of radiation treatment. Of course, I prayed for God to miraculously heal him. This was not God's will.

I also remember praying for my dad to be able to eat an entire meal and not get sick. He loved going to a local restaurant to enjoy their breakfast buffet. On this buffet was bacon, and he LOVED bacon. I questioned how wise it was for him to eat so much bacon because of its high cholesterol and his heart disease. He reminded me he already had cancer and was going to die anyway, so he may as well eat what he wanted! I know we were not related by blood, but I am beginning to think this is where my strange sense of humor might have originated. I learned from an expert! After eating the bacon, eggs, Danish, and fresh fruit, my dad would most often get sick. This sickness was not brought on by over-eating. It was the side effect of radiation.

That's when I prayed he would be able to enjoy that bacon, and God answered that prayer. It was a blessing for me. It was a small request, in some respects, but a big blessing for my dad and me.

I have prayed for cars to start when the engine was making a horrible noise, or no noise at all (don't you sometimes wish we could get around on bicycles?), and I have seen God answer those prayers despite the circumstances of the situation. I once prayed over a stove/range combination my husband and I were installing. It would not slip into the opening in our kitchen. It was about one gazillionth of an inch too wide. I prayed and asked God to allow the stove to slip into place. He did just as I asked. I often wonder if God sometimes tells the angels, "You aren't going to believe her latest request!" However, it would be my guess He finishes that conversation with, "She is so faithful to praise me, as well as ask for help, that I am not offended at all. I think it is great she wants to talk to me about everything!"

Please understand that I am not telling you these stories to honor myself. God is to receive all the honor and praise. I am telling you these stories to help you understand there is not a situation in your life which you are prohibited from bringing to God. For example, every time I walk up or down a flight of stairs, especially if I am carrying something, I ask God to keep me safe. This would not seem strange to you at all if you knew how many accidents I've had. One of my friends calls me "Kamikazi Carol." I am beginning to think it is a good name. I recently stitched all the way through my finger with the sewing machine. Who does this kind of thing? Oh, yeah – ME. That was when I prayed, "God, I know I just did something really stupid, but please take care of my finger. I want to finish this project, and I don't have time for my finger to fall off!" Once again, I think God giggled, shook His head in laughter, and reminded Himself that I am HIS kid, after all. I truly believe God wants to hear from us. He wants to be invited into all aspects of our lives. There is nothing He has posted an "off limits" sign on.

As you might have guessed, praying for the BIG things in life is just a natural occurrence for me. You would think I would not have had too many instances to pray for BIG things, but you would be wrong. I have a friend who once asked me, "Do the people in your family ever have normal illnesses like a sore throat or tonsillitis? It seems they always have unusual illnesses." She was correct. My life has been full of unusual situations that absolutely required a big God to handle.

I remember learning my husband had been in a terrible accident at work. He was rushed by ambulance to a local hospital. I, of course, quickly made my way to meet him in the emergency room. This story would start, however, with our cute little kindergarten daughter, Brandie, replying to the news of her Daddy's accident with, "Momma, we need to say a word prayer." What she meant was a "word of prayer," but in her little tender heart, it meant the same thing. Together we knelt beside the bed, and we prayed together for her Daddy. We did not know the details of his accident, nor did we know how severe his injuries were. We just prayed.

After getting Brandie off to her very last day of kindergarten, I proceeded to the hospital. That was when the second prayer happened. I did not know how to get to this hospital. I had called our minister to see if he could help give me directions, but the hospital to which my husband, Michael, was taken was not one our minister had ever visited. I had a general idea of the location of the hospital, but exact directions were not available. There was no such thing as GPS on my phone, (which, by the way, hung on the wall in the kitchen) so I did what I knew how to do best. I asked my Father for help. Don't you know God guided me directly to the emergency room without a single problem!

The next 18 months were absolutely filled with prayer. My husband had sustained a closed-head injury, and he also had amnesia. (I told you we had unusual things happen in our family.) When he first awoke, he did not remember being married. This was quite a shock. Then, upon my arrival, I realized he did not recognize me. This seemed to clear in his mind, but he did not know how long we had been married, how old our daughter was, where we lived, what the names of our animals were, what kind of car he drove, where he worked, and on and on. If ever I prayed, it was then. Did I pray more then as compared to now? I really don't think so. Prayer is such an important part of my life that constantly calling on Jesus is not something I do just when life throws me a curve ball.

That would be the reason for this book. I have been made aware, as of late, of God's love. More correctly stated, I have been made aware of how little I understand God's love. God loves us so deeply and thoroughly that it is more than we can comprehend. I have learned He wants nothing more than to spend time with us each and every day. He wants us to call upon Him no matter the situation. He is eager to get involved in our lives. We miss out so drastically when we try to handle life on our own effort, strength, and ability. We are so lacking, and He is so able.

In October of 2006, my mother, who was my very heart, was diagnosed with Alzheimer's Disease. I thought my heart would literally break into pieces at the thought of one day losing her. I prayed diligently for her healing, comfort, happiness, and release of pain. That journey of caregiving, and the resulting books, podcasts, videos, not for profit organization, and opportunities to share her story have all been proof of God's blessings upon the prayers I prayed for her. She went to Heaven May 31, 2019, and God sustained me through her homegoing journey, and the grief that followed, in ways I would never have dreamed. I have continued to carry on her legacy through my work as a Certified Dementia Practitioner as I also carry on the legacy of Jesus Christ's work in my life and His sacrifice for me.

Through our study together, we will look at some of the prayers of righteous people in The Bible. We will see God at work. We will also compare their prayers and their circumstances to situations in our lives today. God has not changed how He goes about doing business and answering prayers. Hebrews 13:8 states, *"Jesus Christ is the same yesterday and today and forever."* Those are words that have been trusted for thousands of years, and they are still true today. This same Jesus Christ is eager to lead us straight to His heart. Let's go together!

"The greatest thing anyone can do for God or man is pray."

(S.D. GORDON)

CHAPTER ONE - THE WHAT, WHEN AND WHY OF PRAYER

What

Prayer is simply a conversation with God. Prayer always involves two people, and it ONLY involves two people. These two people are you and God. Even if you are praying before a crowd of thousands, that prayer is a conversation between you and God. I remember listening to men pray aloud in church when I was growing up. In retrospect, I realize my mind was not quite where it should have been. I would count how many times this one particular man said "Our Gracious Heavenly Father." At last count, I think I was pushing over a hundred repetitions, but maybe my count was off. I just knew his type of praying was really bothersome to me.

If you are praying to be heard by others, it is not a prayer. Matthew

6:7-8 tells us *"Do not use meaningless repetition as the Gentiles do, for they suppose that they will be heard for their many words. So do not be like them; for your Father knows what you need before you ask Him."*

Prayer should come from the heart and not the intellect. When we pray from the heart, our communication with God is clear and strong. If there were a signal meter on that type of prayer, as there is on a cell phone, all the bars would be present on the signal strength. When we pray from some place other than the heart, we are praying for a purpose other than having communication with our Father. Sometimes this means we pray so others will hear us. Sometimes we repeat a memorized prayer as a matter of routine. Sometimes our minds are in a totally different place. We need to have our heart and our mind focused on coming before the Almighty God. This is a huge honor and benefit we have been given as children of God.

What makes prayer even more amazing is this. We can access the throne room of grace at any moment of any day. Do you remember Old Testament teaching on the Temple? The high priest was allowed into the inner room of the temple, known as The Holy of Holies, once a year. At that time, he offered a blood sacrifice. This special place was the dwelling place of God among His people. But, I repeat, no one but the high priest could enter. Further, even he could only do so once a year.

We, on the other hand, are allowed to come before God every second of every day. We do not need to enter a special temple, arrive on a special day, or bring a special sacrifice. These necessary requirements were all paid for and supplied by the shedding of Jesus' blood on Calvary. Because of this gift of love on our behalf, we can freely come before the throne. Hear the words of Hebrews 4:14-16. *"Therefore, since we have a great high priest who has passed through the heavens, Jesus the Son of God, let us hold fast our confession. For we do not have a high priest who cannot sympathize with our weaknesses, but One who has been tempted in all things as we are, yet without sin. Therefore, let us draw near with confidence to the throne of grace, so that we may receive mercy and find grace to help in time of need."*

This is proof positive of our ability to seek God's face through Jesus. Prayer is a relaxed and informal conversation with a loving Father that begins with God calling out to us first. I love the thought of God calling me to prayer. I think most of us assume we must call out to God first. However, God is always calling us into conversation with Him. Prayer, therefore, is an intimate relationship between man and God. If all we do is pray at church, we are missing the intimacy of prayer.

Let's recall the story of Paul in Acts chapter 22 when he was still called Saul. He tells of being on the road to Damascus around noontime. A very bright light suddenly flashed from heaven, and Paul fell to the ground. He then heard a voice saying, *"Saul, Saul, why are you persecuting Me?"* (Acts 22:7) Notice how God knew Saul by name. He knew him personally. A similar story is told in Exodus 3:4. Moses was on the job, tending a flock, when an angel of the Lord appeared to him in a blazing fire from a bush. Being curious, Moses went to examine the bush. He noticed the bush was not being consumed by the fire. The Lord noticed Moses investigating the bush, and the Lord said, *"Moses, Moses!"*

God called Paul and Moses by name, and He calls us by name. Why would a loving God not know every detail about His children? It only stands to reason God would call out to us. When He does, He expects a response. That response is known as prayer.

So, what is prayer? It is the means by which we communicate with a loving God. A God who seeks us out, calls us by name, and wants nothing but the best for His children. It is a way for us to tell God of our love for Him, show our affection toward Him, and lay out our desires and needs to Him. It is, also, a way for this same God to communicate with us. He answers ours prayers in many ways. The beautiful aspect of prayer is this: God wants nothing more than to be in communication with His kids. When this communication is frequent and heartfelt, then He has children who are ready, willing, and able to do His work.

When

Prayer is not an "IF you pray" situation, it is a "WHEN you pray" situation. These are the words used in the Sermon on the Mount in Matthew 6. We read in verse 5, "When you pray....," and in verse 6, "when you pray...," and in verse 7, "when you are praying." These verses preface the beautiful words of "The Lord's Prayer" where we are taught HOW to pray. It is clear through reading these verses that we are to pray.

Prayer should not be a temporary state of being; rather, it should be an on-going calling out to the Father. Communication is the most effective way of building a relationship with anyone. God is no exception. Remember, God does not **need** to have a relationship with us, yet He wants one. We, on the other hand, have a strong need to have a relationship with Him. However, because He is a loving God, He seeks us out in order to begin that relationship building process. The thought of "when" we pray is all the more important when we realize our need for God and His desire to keep company with us.

As the scriptures unfold, we learn of many prayers. Let us consider a few more well-known examples. In Genesis chapter 20 we have the story of Abraham deceiving Abimelech. Abraham instructed Sarah to say she was his sister rather than his wife. In actuality, Abraham felt justified in saying this, as Sarah actually was his half-sister. However, in saying this to Abimelech, he placed Abimelech in a position that could have led to sin. Abimelech "took Sarah". God, knowing the situation, kept Abimelech from touching Sarah, and instructed him to return Sarah to Abraham.

Upon the return of Sarah to her husband, Abimelech questioned Abraham, and then offered his land for Abraham to settle wherever he should choose. At this point, Abraham prayed to God, and *"God healed Abimelech, his wife and his maids, so that they bore children. For the Lord had closed fast all the wombs of the household of Abimelech because of Sarah, Abraham's wife."* (Genesis 20:18)

Through this story, we can see God protecting Abimelech from sinning. God called out to Abimelech, helped him to understand the situation, and educated him as to the plan for correction. God also does this in our lives. We may find ourselves involved in a situation in which we never intended to be a part. This situation could lead us to sin. If we are truly listening for God's voice, and seeking to do His will, He will lead us safely through these situations. It is not God's will to see us fail, but He does allow us to experience trying times to see if we will call upon Him and trust Him to bring us through the tough times of life. Jeremiah 29:11 confirms this with these words, *"'For I know the plans that I have for you', declares the Lord, 'plans for welfare and not for calamity, to give you a future and a hope'."*

A real life example may look like this. If you have ever received the wrong change when making a financial transaction, you may have found yourself in a position to sin. Should the change received have been less than what was appropriate, you would have certainly spoken up and sought a solution. However, should the change have been more than was appropriate, you very well might have found yourself in a position that could have led to sin.

While I would never suppose to say God intentionally placed that extra money in your hand as a test, I do believe that could sometimes be the case. Whether He is testing us, or whether the situation is merely human error, we are faced with the opportunity to either sin or show strength of character. In these situations, God will always be seeking a time of conversation with us. He will certainly be available to help us understand the situation and give us guidance as to how it should properly be handled. This is similar to the situation in which Abimelech found himself. May we be found acting as wisely as Abimelech.

What other life situations should call us to prayer? The answer is, ALL life situations should call us to prayer. Those situations may be times of financial need, physical need, emotional need, spiritual need, or any need. Those situations may be times of joy or celebration. Those situations may be times spent offering praise and adoration to God. In actuality, there is never a time that prayer is not appropriate. Yes, you may not find it easy to pray aloud at any given moment, but a prayer offered in the quietness of the heart is always heard by God. After all, even Jesus found prayer a necessity.

It may seem strange to think of Jesus praying. To whom did He pray? Why did He even need to pray? Jesus prayed to God – His Father. We read in Mark 1:35, *"In the early morning, while it was still dark, Jesus got up, left the house, and went away to a secluded place, and was praying there."* Many people use this verse as their inspiration to spend time with God in the early morning hours. I think this is a wonderful idea and a great example to follow. However, I find my most meaningful time with The Father is in the late morning hours. I love to feel the sun streaming in my lanai while I join God for our time together. It is a great comfort to think of Him waiting for me to enter His presence. He is there waiting on me to join Him.

So, why did Jesus need to pray? He needed conversation with His Father, just as we need conversation with our Heavenly Father. Jesus had taken on the form of man. Even though He was still God the Son, He desired communication with God The Father. Think of that. If Jesus, who was perfect, needed time in prayer with God, it would seem we would need this same communication all the more.

Luke 5:16 tells us that Jesus would often slip away to the wilderness to pray. He needed time alone. If you try to pray with the television going, the cell phone nearby, or any of a thousand other ways to be interrupted, your time with God is made less effective. Set aside a time that you are not disturbed by the outside influences of life. It is perfectly acceptable to turn the cell phone and television off and put a "do not disturb" sign on the front door. God will bless your time with Him just as surely as He blessed Jesus' time with Him.

Why

I have a daughter. I love to hear from her several times each day. We don't always have important issues to discuss, but I still like to hear her voice. Do you think God is any different? Do you think He is annoyed when we call on Him for incidental, inconsequential things? No, of course He is not. He is honored to hear from us. He wants to help us think things through. Or, maybe we are calling on Him to celebrate. Oh, that is joy to His ears, also. We are experts at calling on God when life is easy and the sun is shining, but when life gets difficult, and the storm rolls in, do we remember God?

Still the question is asked, "Why should we pray?" Mark 10:27 answers this quite succinctly, in my opinion. *"Looking at them, Jesus said, 'With people it is impossible, but not with God; for all things are possible with God'."* WOW! That is certainly reason enough to pray. We serve a great big God. There is never, and there never will be, a situation that is more than He can handle. Further, He will never be taken by surprise. When the lab reports show a disease, when the family income is lost, when the best friend betrays you, never will God stop and say, "I wasn't expecting that! What am I going to do now?" If He did, this book would be totally pointless. Who wants a God that is not in total control?

I have recently been made aware of one of my personality traits. I am a Type A personality. I like timeliness, order, and I like to be in charge. I believe we would all be better off if life offered black and white choices. In my opinion, the "grey" areas just lead to confusion. Sometimes I think I should have joined the military so that life could have been led by a fixed set of rules! That would explain why I absolutely need a God who is big enough to handle whatever I throw at Him.

I once attended a seminar given by a local hospice organization. The minister speaking that day told the story of his father dying. When a friend asked him "John, are you doing OK?" John replied, "No, I am NOT doing OK. In fact if Jesus Christ were standing right in front of me this very minute, I would punch his eyes out." At first glance you might find his response to be rude, disrespectful, and just plan WRONG. However, listen to the response John received from his friend.

"John, I am so glad to hear you say that. That shows you have a God big enough to handle your anger and love you right through it." That is such an amazing thought. God is not revolted by our anger. He wants to help us through that anger.

Do you remember what Job went through? He lost everything. He cried out to God in his anger and grief. Job 19:17-22 records Job's anger. *"My breath is offensive to my wife, and I am loathsome to my own brothers. Even young children despise me; I rise up and they speak against me. All my associates abhor me, and those I love have turned against me. My bone clings to my skin and my flesh, and I have escaped only by the skin of my teeth. Pity me, pity me, O you my friends, for the hand of God has struck me. Why do you persecute me as God does, and are not satisfied with my flesh?"* Job was crying out in his pain.

David, in Psalm 10 cried, *"Why do You stand afar off, O Lord? Why do you hide Yourself in times of trouble?"* These two men were Godly men who were experiencing times of extreme sorrow. They cried out to God, and they didn't hold anything back.

I have always loved the verse in James 4:3 that reads, *"You ask and do not receive, because you ask with wrong motives."* That verse will never be my downfall. You see, I ask for EVERYTHING. I pray that my motives are pure and holy, and I am sure I have failed in that respect. However, I truly believe I should take all my concerns, joys, sorrows, pleasures, pains, whatever I am experiencing to God. I thank Him when I feel good, and I also pray while experiencing aches and pains. I have talked with God about heartburn, menstrual cramps, and migraines. Was I pleased to have these afflictions? Absolutely not. Further, I made sure I expressed that to my Father. He didn't mind hearing my heart one bit. In fact, being able to express my pain makes me all the more excited to be able to express my joy.

In looking at the question "Why should we pray?," the answer could be explained through James 5:16. Listen now, *"Therefore, confess your sins to one another, and pray for one another so that you may be healed. The effective prayer of a righteous man can accomplish much."* My guess is you are wondering about the "righteous man" part and deciding you are not "righteous" enough to have your prayers answered. However, we need to look at what it means to be righteous. Righteousness is not a measure of how moral a person is. It has nothing to do with the keeping of a certain list of standards. We are righteous people because we have accepted the grace offered through the shedding of Christ's blood. By understanding this, we can have confidence in our authority to come before the Throne of God with our requests.

This scripture also teaches us to pray for one another. This is a direct command. It is not a suggestion. If you are not vested enough in the life of other people, and have a desire for their well-being, your life is out of balance. Part of the wonder and beauty of being human is the ability to have sympathy for others. When we care enough for someone else that we take their concerns to God, we experience the joy of God's presence in our life and in their life, also. It is a double reward.

A very compelling reason to pray is found in the parable of the widow who continually came to a certain judge asking for protection from her opponent. After she persisted, the judge finally conceded. These are The Lord's words. *"Now, will not God bring about justice for His elect who cry to Him day and night, and will He delay long over them. I tell you that He will bring justice for them quickly. However, when the Son of Man comes, will He find faith on the earth?"* (Luke 18:7-8)

"Will He find faith on the earth?" is an important and disturbing question. This should make us search our souls. Do our actions reflect the goodness of God? Does our life show others that our trust is placed in God and not in man? If the answer is "no," then we should follow the instructions in this passage to "cry to Him day and night." This crying out will only bring us closer to God. When this is achieved, our thoughts will turn to Him and His ways continually. It is hard to forget a gracious, loving, all-powerful God when you have just experienced a personal daily visitation with this same God.

Ephesians 6:18 tell us, *"With all prayer and petition, pray at all times in the Spirit, and with this in view, be on the alert with all perseverance and petition for all the saints..."* Once again we are told to pray. This praying is to be done "in the Spirit." This would take us back to our earlier thoughts on prayer being a conversation between you and God. It is not so others may hear your beautifully constructed sentences. Praying to God for the express purpose of hearing His answer and revealing your heart would certainly be praying in the Spirit.

Notice how we are instructed, once again, to make petition for all the saints. Pray for each other. It is a scriptural teaching, and it is a wonderful way to grow closer to our neighbors and closer to God. Let us not, however, over-look the "pray at all times" part of this passage. How is it possible to pray while working, attending school, driving, or doing any of the multiple activities we are called to do in life? Sometimes the best prayers are those that are quietly spoken from the heart. They are not verbalized for anyone to hear. God knows the heart, understands the groanings of the heart, and answers those prayers.

There is great comfort in Romans 8:26 - *"In the same way the Spirit also helps our weakness; for we do not know how to pray as we should, but the Spirit Himself intercedes for us with groanings too deep for words."* When life has you in tears, take those tears to God. The Spirit can deliver those tears to the Father as words of petition on your behalf. Maybe those tears are tears of joy. The Spirit is still there to intercede for us. It matters not the reason for our silent, heartfelt conversation with God. It matters that we come to Him, acknowledge He is God, and honor Him by making our heart available to Him.

Scripture teaches us how God is honored when we ask for big

things. Just as parents want to do good things for their children, so God wants to do good things for His children. His desire, however, is so much deeper than our humanness can imagine. Because of this, God is not offended when we seek Him. He wants us to experience the closeness that is a result of a consistent prayer life with Him.

We have looked at the "what, when, and why" of prayer. All of our spiritual wellness is built around the need for constant communication with our Father. There is nothing that will benefit us more than seeking God daily. There is nothing that will cause us to lack more than not having this communication with God.

Prayer is not a suggestion. Pray is a command given to us in scripture. If you find prayer to be difficult, tell God your concern. He will come to you in such a special way that praying to Him will be as natural as talking to anyone else you love. Don't spend one minute trying to use "holy" words. Just talk to God with the same words you would use to talk to the next person who rings your phone. This will make communication natural and pleasant. Give God a call today. He is waiting on you!

The "why" of prayer is to help bring God into focus, His power, His character, His love, His grace, and His mercy. It is also used to take us further away from the self-centeredness of the human personality. That is why prayer must be an intimate relationship between us and God. This intimacy is the only way to achieve the goals and the purposes of prayer.

"God shapes the world by prayer. The more prayer there is in the world, the better the world will be. The mightier the forces against evil."

CHAPTER TWO - HOW DO I KNOW GOD HEARS MY PRAYERS?

Praying and faith are two things that go together. One without the other is useless. If our prayers are not accompanied by faith that God hears and answers prayers, then what is the use in praying? If we have faith, but have no access to God in whom are we placing our faith, what is the purpose of prayer?

We will look at several scriptures that tell us God hears and answers prayer. It is not a concept, instead it is a reality. However, belief that prayer is answered is best achieved by the practicing of prayer and the seeking of answers.

God always answers every prayer. Sometimes the answer is yes, or no, or yes – maybe later, or wait. We may be thrilled with His answer, or we may be disappointed in His answer. There have been times when I prayed and God gave me exactly what I asked. There have been times when God gave me more than I asked. There have been times when God did not give me what I asked at all.

It Was Not What I Expected

Let's look at the times when the answer was less than was expected. This will allow us to finish this chapter with the more pleasant stories of wonderfully beautiful answers to prayer. There have been times in my life when I prayed fervently for a specific request only to have God deny the answer. Looking back on that request, I now see the thing I wanted was not good for me. Not knowing this at the time, my mind was focused on getting the desired answer. God's mind, however, was focused on doing what was best for His child.

In my twenties, my parents divorced. They had been married twenty-eight years. I can so vividly recall begging God to bring my parents back together. What I did not know was my mother was suffering from physical, sexual, and mental abuse at the hands of my father. This was a terrible situation for her, and she was being destroyed minute by minute. The reconciliation never took place. I realized God was protecting my mother from a future of what would have been horror. God loved me and my mother enough to say "no" to my prayer. I am thankful He did.

In First Samuel we read of the elders demanding Samuel appoint a king over Israel. Their request was displeasing to Samuel, so Samuel prayed to the Lord regarding their request. God answered Samuel with instructions to explain how the king would be evil and bring about great harm to all the people. Upon learning this information, the people did not believe Samuel's words from God. Still they demanded a king. God granted their request. The king, of course, was evil just as God had told them he would be.

From this we see God does not always answer our prayers with "yes – you may have exactly what you ask for." In this story, however, He did use the opportunity to teach a lesson to the people. It was a tough lesson, indeed. Trusting in God enough to accept His "no" answer is difficult. Often we are certain we know what is best for us. However, we only see part of the picture, and God sees the entire picture. His "no" is often the beginning of a beautiful "yes" yet to come.

Now that we have looked at the less pleasant answers to prayer, let us take a look at answers that are more pleasant. If we are questioning whether God **hears** our prayers, the obvious way to determine this would be if God **answers** our prayers. Hebrews 4:16 states, *"Therefore let us draw near with confidence to the throne of grace, so that we may receive mercy and find grace to help in time of need."*

It is the drawing near with confidence part that most catches my attention. I John 5:14-15 elaborates this point. *"This is the confidence which we have before Him, that if we ask anything according to His will, He hears us, and if we know that He hears us in whatever we ask, we know that we have the requests which we have asked from Him."*

It Was Better Than I Could Have Ever Dreamed

Throughout my life, I have called on God for every kind of situation you can imagine. I truly believe He is honored by my constant contact with Him and my constant asking of Him. I would like to relate a couple of very specific instances of my asking.

After trying to start a family for quite some time, I was pleased to hear the news I was pregnant. My husband and I were so excited to begin our family. Because my pregnancy occurred while using fertility drugs, my doctor advised me to have a hormone level test every Monday for many weeks. The ideal situation would show the hormone level in my blood increasing weekly. Everything went just as we had hoped for several weeks.

Then, on a Friday, the dreaded news came through. My hormone level had dropped drastically, and I was expected to miscarry the baby over the weekend. My heart was broken. How could this be happening? This began a series of events that I will never forget. My husband and I cried out to God with our pain. We cried out to each other. We could do absolutely nothing to stop the death of this little person inside of me, and we so desperately wanted to do so. All we could do was pray.

Now that is a strange statement when you actually think about things. "All we could do was pray?" Is there anything more powerful than prayer to the Almighty God? Yet, we hear people use this very phrase in relation to stressful events in their lives. Imagine where we would be without that ability to pray. That is something my mind cannot and will not grasp.

So, we prayed more diligently than we ever had in our lives. On Monday I returned to have the blood drawn just as I had the previous weeks. The doctor was surprised to see I was still pregnant. On Thursday of that week, the doctor called with the most unexpected news. He said, "Carol, I can't explain it. Your hormone level is exactly where it should be for the number of weeks pregnant you are. Your baby is fine, and everything looks good for the future." Oh my goodness! You cannot believe the excitement and joy and praise and tears I experienced at that very moment. I was at work when I received the news, and everyone around me thought something horrific had happened. I could not wait to call my husband to share the news. God had answered our prayers in a mighty and wonderful way!

Fast forward some 36 years later, and that same sweet baby was about to become a mother. However, this journey was wrought with more emotional pain than any couple should ever experience. At age fourteen, my daughter was told she could never conceive because of an abnormality in her reproductive organs. Further, the doctor's told her if she did conceive, she and the baby would most likely die. As a result, our kids went through three rounds of IVF to form a family. On their third round of IVF, a baby began to grow in the womb of a surrogate. In case you are a little rusty on gestation and the process, when a baby makes it to 13 weeks gestation, the chances of miscarriage drop dramatically.

It was the thirteenth week that our worlds were forever changed. The baby unexpectedly died. Tests were done on this wonderful new life, a baby girl, and nothing was wrong with her. She just died. If I could tell you the pain we felt, it would not truly cover it. However, the pain my kids felt losing this hope of their baby girl was enough to make me literally ache. "Why, OH GOD, did this happen? What is your plan? HELP!!!"

About one year later, the kids had gone through a couple more rounds of IVF, and they were waiting on an appropriate surrogate to carry the embryo. There seemed to be no one available. I was praying so diligently. Then, one day, I heard God say, "Don't limit me." I thought, "Well, Okay, God, but what does that mean?" It was then I knew. Brandie would have a baby on her own. No surrogate.

I began watching and observing my girl, and I knew she was pregnant. I told my husband my thoughts, and he said, "She better not be! That would not be good news." Oh, but **GOD**! God changed everything in her story and in our lives.

I sit here now the "Grammy" for baby Tessa, and she is perfect. (I know, you think your grandkids are perfect, too, but, ...). What's more, her Momma came through her pregnancy and delivery like a champ. God had a plan. Was it what we expected? Nope, not even close. Was it 10,000 times better? Absolutely!

It is stories like this that make me KNOW, without one doubt whatsoever, God not only hears, but He answers prayers. He wants what is best for His children. He is so honored when we call upon Him, lay out all the feelings in our heart, and trust Him to take all those feelings and make something wonderful from them.

Listen to these beautiful words in Luke. *"So I say to you, "ask, and it will be given to you; seek and you will find; knock, and it will be opened to you. For everyone who asks, receives; and he who seeks, finds; and to him who knocks, it will be opened."*

I like the rest of this passage, also. *"Now suppose one of you fathers is asked by his son for a fish; he will not give him a snake instead of a fish, will he? Or if he is asked for an egg, he will not give him a scorpion will he? If you then, being evil, know how to give good gifts to your children, how much more will your heavenly Father give the Holy Spirit to those who ask Him?"* I believe God is honored when we ask for **BIG** things and ʟɪᴛᴛʟᴇ things. I believe He is honored when we ask specifically. After all, I don't want a snake or a scorpion!

Prayers Of Petition

Now that we have discussed asking God for our needs, while

having a heart that believes He not only hears but answers prayer, it would be good to identify that prayer. This type of prayer is a prayer of petition. According to freedictionary.com, a petition is "A solemn supplication or request to a superior authority". That seems to be an excellent explanation of what we are doing when we come before God with our requests. While it may seem selfish to constantly come before God with requests for others as well as ourselves, it is actually a scriptural act.

Philippians 4:6-7 states, *"Be anxious for nothing, but in everything by prayer and supplication with thanksgiving let your requests be made known to God. And the peace of God, which surpasses all comprehension, will guard your hearts and your minds in Christ Jesus."* It is clear we are instructed to bring "everything by prayer" before God.

While seeking God for everything, we need to come before Him with thanksgiving and faith. The words of Matthew 6:25-34 tell us we have no reason to worry over anything. We are instructed that worrying about what we shall eat, drink, wear, sow, reap, or gather into barns is not necessary. If God clothes the grass of the field, which is green today and dead tomorrow, wouldn't it stand to reason He would clothe us? The scripture then dramatically says, *"You of little faith!"*

The words that follow instruct us not to worry over any of these things because God already knows of our need. So what should we be concentrating our thoughts on? We are told to seek first His kingdom and His righteousness. After doing this, all the needed things will be added to us.

We all worry. We worry about a myriad of items. We worry about food, clothes, tomorrow, good times (because bad times must be around the corner), cataclysmic events, finances, jobs, kids, and family. At least a thousand more items could be added to the list.

This results in both physical and mental problems. This worrying does not bring us one bit closer to God and the love He has for us.

If, instead of worry, we were seeking the fruits of the Spirit – love, joy, peace, patience, kindness, goodness, faithfulness, gentleness, and self-control – then our hearts and minds would be so absorbed with the goodness of God, there would be no room for worry. Allowing even a corner of our brain to be doubtful allows worry to return. We are most blessed when we leave all of life's situations in God's hands.

Oh, how easy it is to write those words. Oh, how difficult it is, on the other hand, to live those words out. I can tell you from personal experience, the scriptures are true. If we are spending time with the Father daily, through prayer and scripture study, our minds are more likely to recall His words and seek His face than if we are not continually seeking Him.

Think of the friend you see every day. You will often remember something they might have said that stuck in your mind. The more you visit with this friend, the more likely you are to have a stockpile of sayings or thoughts from this friend. If, on the other hand, you only see this friend on Christmas and Easter (as so many people do when they visit church twice a year), what is the likelihood of remembering a specific phrase months after the event?

When times are tough and the soul needs encouragement, we need a reservoir of God's words to pull on. We need to be reminded of His mercy and goodness. We need to know, beyond any doubt, God hears and answers prayer.

Hi Honey, I'm Home!

I told you the story of my husband's accident and injury to his brain. After going through 18 months of rehabilitation, the company he worked for placed him in a job they knew full well he was not capable of doing. His doctor interceded on his behalf, but the company stood strong. He worked this job to the best of his ability but was eventually "laid off." That is a new term for fired. He was actually escorted out of the building one day, and he wasn't given any notice that it was about to happen. He was not allowed to remove his lunch from his desk or take personal belongings from his office. He was escorted out the door by a member of the company's security staff.

Upon arriving home, Michael knocked on the door, as I had locked the storm door. When I opened it and saw him standing there, I was surprised. That was when I learned he was no longer employed. At that point, I had been operating a small cleaning company for several years. He told me he would begin sending out resumes immediately. I recommended he start cleaning with me the very next day.

I can honestly say I was not worried one bit about our future. No, we didn't have a nice steady income any longer. We also didn't have the fabulous health insurance we had come to depend on. We only had the income I made by cleaning three houses a week, and we had no health insurance whatsoever. No more contributions to retirement plans. No more matched savings. No more security. It **seemed** all of that was true. The facts were quite different.

After one week of Michael working with me, I am excited to say God supplied us with fourteen new customers. We were steadily cleaning two houses per day. It was during this time we discovered we were really good as a team in this business of cleaning houses. We prayed and asked God's continued blessings on this small business. We worked up to cleaning four or five houses every day.

We never once missed a payment on one thing. We even still enjoyed the fun of eating out. I don't mean to heap praises on our heads. What I want to convey is the peace that infiltrated our lives because we knew God was absolutely in control of everything. At that point in our lives, we often felt God was "showing off" by blessing us so big. We continued working together for a total of twelve years. It was at this time we began to pray for a "regular" job for Michael.

That is another story of God's answer to prayer. I had great concerns as to what would be a good fit for Michael considering he did have issues from his brain injury. After several months of praying by both of us, I knew God had given me an answer in regards to this "regular" job we were seeking. However, because I believe God isn't bothered by such a request, I asked God to give Michael this same vision. Further, I asked God to have Michael bring this vision to me as confirmation we were doing His will.

One day while driving   in Rock Hill, South Carolina (our hometown), Michael said, "I know exactly where I want to work." My heart was in my throat. When he told me, I remember having cold chills from head to toe. It was then I told him of my conversations with God. I explained that I had been aware of this job choice for several weeks, and I had even asked God to lay it on his heart and mind, also. We both became so excited to pursue this new opportunity for our lives!

I know you are not surprised to hear he obtained the job without issue. He worked this job for two years, and he was extremely successful. However, it was through this job he learned more of his strengths. He was busy learning about the "new Michael" that had emerged as a result of his accident. We both were very aware of his need for a different job. Guess what we did! We prayed!

One important note to this story is the economic recession in which we were living. Our entire country was seeing a huge downturn in employment. People were losing their jobs in record numbers. Companies were closing, and unemployment lines were growing. Then, to top things off, we asked God for a new job in the midst of all of this chaos. Do you think God was shocked by our request? Do you think He thought, "Why can't you be happy with the job you have?" Because I lived through this, I know God was pleased to hear our request. The wonderful news was He was even more pleased to grant our request.

While cleaning for one of our weekly customers, I was approached with the question, "What would it take for Michael to quit his job and come to work for us?" This client's husband was a veterinarian who owned a local animal hospital. My quick (and probably not so smart) response was, "Not much. He is really ready for a change." Through God's divine plan for our lives, Michael began working at this animal hospital, and he worked there over eight years. He would never have guessed he would be led to do this type of work. However, he has stated many times how very much he enjoyed his work. He even said, "If I had tons of money, I would still get up and go to work at the animal hospital." I was thrilled he felt that way because I would stay in bed!

You see, God answers prayers regarding any and all situations. He knows what the answer is before we even ask. We are given His blessings in our lives even when we don't ask. How much more blessed we are when we have been given the opportunity to both ask and receive God's blessings. These blessings are so much sweeter and have a greater impact on our lives.

Don't hesitate to talk to God about whatever your petition is. It absolutely does not matter. You may need to talk to him about your job, your health, your family member who has problems, your addiction, your finances, your car that isn't running correctly, the furnace that is old, the pet who is sick, or the hopes you have in your heart. Whatever the need or desire, take it to God. Give Him the opportunity to "show off" for you. It is a great way to experience Him in a way you will never forget.

As further proof of God's desire to hear and answer prayer, let's see another scripture that supports these thoughts. (If you cannot find scripture that backs up what you believe, you should rethink what you believe.) Look at Malachi 3:10. *"'Bring the whole tithe into the storehouse, so that there may be food in My house, and test Me now in this,' says the Lord of hosts, 'if I will not open for you the windows of heaven and pour out for you a blessing until it overflows.'"*

Now you are talking! Blessings that overflow will certainly be proof positive that God hears and answers prayers. No, every prayer may not be answered exactly as you might think it should be. God, however, knows what is best, and He can't wait to bless you big time!

"Don't pray when you feel like it. Have an
appointment with the Lord and keep it.
A man is powerful on his knees."

(CORRIE TEN BOOM)

CHAPTER THREE - I WAS BIT BY A BAT, AND I PRAYED ABOUT THAT

I n talking with people about the writing of this book, I was shocked to learn of a disturbing commonality among people. It seems there are many people who do not pray for themselves. I have been amazed at this information, and I often felt sad for them. To think of living life without talking to God about every little detail is a horrible thought. I am not ashamed to admit being very dependent upon constant communication with my Father. This makes me excited to write this chapter. I hope it will open up a new way of thinking about prayer that will bring you closer to God and afford you blessings in abundance.

It's A Matter Of The Heart

When we pray for ourselves, this type of prayer is called a prayer of "supplication" or "petition." The word "supplication" is found often in The Bible, and many times it is synonymous with the word "prayer" itself. We are using it in this study to refer to a prayer that is made on behalf of someone or ourselves. Particular to this chapter, we will look at a prayer of supplication as an example of going before God with a request specific for ourselves.

When we are praying with supplication, it would be as a result of a need in our lives. This need causes us to seek God's will and wisdom. We are encouraged and strengthened by communion with God regarding this situation, and we are promised He will hear and work in our lives as a result of the situation. This coming before God requires our hearts to be humble and submissive to the power, goodness, and will of God.

We must have the right "heart attitude" before asking for our requests. Solomon described such a situation in I Kings 8:33. The people were to come before God and make supplication AFTER they had turned to God and confessed His name. The heart attitude is important. In Psalms we read of David saying the Lord had heard his supplication and his voice of weeping. (Psalms 6:8-9) This would show a broken heart ready to be used by God.

If our heart attitude is one that feels we can handle the situation on our own efforts, what would we have the need to come before God to begin with? It is only through the realization of our need, and our belief of God's ability to overcome our inability, we can offer a proper prayer of supplication. This type of praying, just as with all types of praying, is more easily achieved when practiced regularly. It is through the working of God in our hearts that we begin to hear, see, and understand God's work in our every day-to-day events, cares, concerns, or situations.

Asking God for a specific desire of our heart is scriptural. In Mark 10 we read of the blind man named Bartimaeus who was sitting by the side of the road. He heard Jesus of Nazareth approaching him. He cried out, *"Jesus, Son of David, have mercy on me."* (Don't you think it is interesting that this blind man knew it was Jesus coming his way?) Jesus asked him, *"What do you want Me to do for you?"* I really like the blind man's response. He didn't hesitate or mutter or search for words. He boldly and loudly proclaimed, *"Rabonni, I want to regain my sight!"* Was Jesus offended by this direct request for healing? Let's read the scripture and take our answer from there.

"And Jesus said to him, 'Go, your faith has made you well.' Immediately he regained his sight and began following Him on the road." (Mark 10:51-52) This blind man pointedly asked Jesus for the healing of his eyes, and Jesus responded with just the result the man was seeking. Notice the man did not ask for "healing." He asked specifically for his vision. He didn't say, "Well, I sure would like to feel better." No, he said exactly what was on his mind. It was no surprise to Jesus that Bartimaeus was blind. So, it was no surprise to Jesus that Bartimaeus wanted his sight. What logical reason would there be for Bartimaeus to have pretended the loss of his sight was not an issue of importance to him? He wanted to see, and he told Jesus just that.

I remember a childhood story of the man who died and went to heaven. When he entered the pearly gates, he was given a tour of the splendor of heaven. I believe it was Peter who led the tour. After seeing mansions, streets of gold, meeting saints of old, reuniting with loved ones, and, most importantly, meeting his Savior, Peter took this man to a room filled with wonderfully wrapped gifts. The man asked, "What are all these gifts?" Saint Peter responded, "These are all the things God had to give you, and you never asked for them."

That is quite a thought. We struggle through so many situations in life when we should have given those struggles to God and accepted the gifts He had to give us. I may be guilty of many things in my life, but there will not be a room filled with things I didn't ask for when I get to heaven. I ask for everything. And I do mean EVERYTHING.

I truly believe there is nothing God doesn't want to talk with us about. If you learn nothing else through the reading of this book, please understand God's great desire to be in conversation with you. His heart is yearning to have you answer the knock on your door and invite Him in to your life. How do you invite Him? Scripture tell us in Romans 10:9, *"If you declare with your mouth, 'Jesus is Lord,' and believe in your heart that God raised him from the dead, you will be saved."* Oh my friend, if you have never asked Christ into your heart, this will prayer will be the most important prayer you ever speak. Pray with me.

"Dear Father, I thank you for loving me. I thank you for being God. I thank you for sending your Son to die for me. I thank you that He rose from the dead. I ask you to come into my life and feel my heart with your love. I want to serve you, Lord."

It is that easy to pray and ask God to be your Savior. Congratulations! Now the doors are open for all the prayers you will be offering in the days to come.

May I take a personal moment here? (Yes, I know this entire book is a "personal moment!") I have previously written several books. The first book was a 90 day devotional that started out as a personal journal between God and me. After reflection and prayer time, I felt called to make it into a devotional book. It was a blessing to see how God would work with me to bring the daily devotions to a point that anyone who read them would understand my thoughts.

While finishing that book, I was impressed by God with the idea of taking care of His temple. I then began writing the second book, *If My Body Is A Temple, Why Am I Eating Doughnuts?* My reason for telling you this is to honor God. Each and every time I sat at my desk to work on a book, I prayed and asked God to please give me the words He wanted written. I do not have the ability to write one sentence without His putting the thoughts, scriptures, words, sentences, paragraphs, and pages together. Throughout the years, I have written seven books. The majority of them are about dementia caregiving and preventing dementia. (I am unashamed to plug my work, so go to www.letstalkdementia to learn more.)

I am always totally amazed when my time writing with God is over for the day. Some days He gives me thoughts to research, and some days He pours ten pages through my fingers at the computer keyboard. I do not accept any praise for having produced these books or the one you are presently reading. I absolutely know they are the books God and I wrote together. When we meet each day, I ask Him, " please be with me as we work on OUR BOOK today." I so totally enjoy hearing His voice, and it is exciting to know He is using me to bring about something good in my life and in the lives of others. He honors my time with Him each day in this very tangible way. Ane he does the same thing for you. Just invite Him in to every aspect of your day. Be BOLD and ask for His help. He likes to hear from you!

Quite some time ago, there was a popular little book called *The Prayer of Jabez,* by Bruce Wilkinson. It is a great book to read. The story of Jabez can be found in I Chronicles 4:9-10. Two little verses, but they have a huge meaning to me. Jabez prayed to God and asked him to *"enlarge my border, and that Your hand might be with me, and that You would keep me from harm that it may not pain me."* Jabez knew what he wanted, and he wasn't embarrassed or hesitant to ask God for what his heart desired. Listen to the remainder of verse ten. *"And God granted him what he requested."* Isn't that just about the neatest thing in the world? Jabez trusted God enough to lay out his heart before God, and God loved Jabez enough that He granted him what he requested! That, my friend, is a great story. What made Jabez different from most of us today? He trusted God, and he had faith in God. This trust and faith came through a daily walk with God. Sounds like something we should all be working on!

So Tell Me About The Bat

You may be wondering why this chapter is titled "I Was Bit By a Bat, and I Prayed About That." Do you remember me saying my family has a way of having unusual things happen   and unusual illnesses along the way? Well, this story would not be an exception to that rule.

While working for a client one day, I reached into a trash can to pick up one lone piece of trash – a tissue. My intent was to place it in my collection bag. Instead, that tissue was covering a bat that bit the center of my hand! I yelled to my husband (in the South we yell instead of scream), "I just got bit by a bat!" Of course, he responded with, "Just get your work done, woman!" Such sympathy is moving to the core, to say the least.

I then proceeded to run toward him and show him the bat clinging to my hand. "Look, I really did get bit by a bat." By this point, the bat had let go of my hand, and I flung him to the floor. My husband gathered the bat in a plastic bag, tied the bag shut, and placed him in the trash can. Later that day, my dog had an appointment with his veterinarian. I just casually mentioned the bat incident from earlier in the day. The doctor stopped cold in his tracks. "I want that bat." I was shocked he was so adamant about wanting a bat. After all, who wants a bat?

Of course I inquired as to why he wanted the bat. That was when I learned I could have been exposed to rabies. Further, it is unusual for a healthy bat to bite someone. Excuse me! Did he just say rabies? I knew the treatment for rabies exposure could be painful, and I was more than a little frightened.

My husband returned to the "scene of the crime" and obtained the bat. The bat was sent to our local "place where you send bats for checking for rabies," and my family and I waited to see if I had been exposed. See, I told you strange things happen to my family. Of course, we prayed. You see, God already knew about the bat incident. He knew how we would respond, and He was standing beside us through every step of the way. I am happy to report the bat was not rabid, and I suffered no ill consequences from the event. In looking back, I am wondering if God wasn't giving me a really good story for this book. You have to admit, it is strange!

No, you will not always get exactly what you ask for. However, you will always get God's undivided attention when you approach Him with a heartfelt desire to be with Him. That is the best answer, anyway. Scripture does teach us, however, that faith is necessary to please Him. We must come to God and believe that *"He is a rewarder of those who seek Him."* (Hebrews 11:6) If we present ourselves to God and believe in His divinity, power, strength, grace, mercy, and love, we have placed ourselves in a position to hear from Heaven. When this is practiced on a daily basis, life's curve balls are just little blips on the radar screen.

I do not mean to make light of any pain, suffering, or hard trial you may be experiencing. Truly, some of life's experiences are a great deal more than a "blip." When we leave that tough time at the feet of Jesus, then we begin to see why this daily walk with Him is so important. *"Come to Me, all who are weary and heavy laden, and I will give you rest."* In this woman's opinion, that sums this chapter up quite nicely!

"Talking to men for God is a great thing, but
talking to God for men is greater still."

(E.M. BOUNDS)

CHAPTER FOUR - PRAYING FOR OTHERS

Praying for others is such an important part of our prayer life. These prayers are called prayers of intercession. This type of prayer is an act of love on behalf of the person for whom we are praying. Caring enough about another person so their needs are forefront in our mind means we are interceding for them. We are asking God specifically to work in their life in a way which benefits them.

There will be many times in our lives when we pray for others. It is easy to recognize our need to pray for the sick, the family who has lost a loved one, the poor, or the weak. However, there is no end to the variety of requests we might make known to God on behalf of others. Interestingly, we do not have to agree with someone to intercede for them. We can pray on their behalf even if we are not necessarily on their side. If our heart is truly seeking that which is most beneficial for that person, God honors our heart.

Do we always get the answer we are looking for? That would certainly depend on how we go about this prayer of intercession. We cannot understand or predict God's plans and purposes. We only see a small glimpse of the picture. *"For now we see in a mirror dimly, but then face to face; now I know in part, but then I will know fully just as I also have been fully known."* (I Corinthians 13:12)

There is so much about life we cannot understand. Sometimes what we seek simply does not fit into God's plans. We must learn to accept this as what is best for everyone involved. As mentioned previously, sometimes God answers prayers with "No." That "no" is the best answer we could receive. We must remember God has HIS plans. However, maybe the purpose of certain intercessory prayers is to change the one **doing** the praying. Maybe we are being taught how to love more fully and to look at other's needs more than our own needs. This result of intercessory praying may not be at all what we expected, but we are made stronger because of its answer.

What If I Don't Want To Pray For Them?

There have been times in all our lives when it was difficult to pray for someone who abused or mistreated us. Samuel said in I Samuel 12:23-24, *"Far be it from me that I should sin against the Lord by ceasing to pray for you....fear the Lord and serve Him in truth with all your heart; for consider what great things He has done for you."* When we consider all the blessings in our lives, we absolutely have no good reason not to pray for those who are difficult.

Don't forget the words of The Beatitudes. *"Blessed are you when people insult you and persecute you, and falsely say all kinds of evil against you because of Me. Rejoice and be glad, for your reward in heaven is great; for in the same way they persecuted the prophets who were before you."* (Matthew 5:11-12) Now that is one more big challenge. It is through practice that we perfect this act of intercession. It is through practice that we also receive the blessings of intercession.

Abraham Was Wheeling And Dealing!

The scriptures are full of stories of intercession. Abraham had quite a lengthy conversation with God regarding the number of righteous people in Sodom. God was going to destroy Sodom unless Abraham could find fifty righteous people. Now Abraham began to be worried about this deal. He started asking God to reduce the number in increments of five. *"Suppose the fifty righteous are lacking five, will You destroy the whole city because of five?"* (Genesis 18:28)

Abraham interceded for Sodom until God agreed to save them if Abraham could find ten righteous people. God was not offended by Abraham's continual pleading with Him. Rather, God was pleased to be in conversation with Abraham. The same is true of us today. We need to learn to speak with God in our own language, using the vernacular of our day, and expressing the feelings of our heart. He is willing and excited to listen.

If you want to look at an example of interceding for someone while they are being persecuted, we must look at Stephen. We learn in Acts 7 of Stephen's death by stoning. During the process, Stephen cried out *"Lord, do not hold this sin against them?"* (Acts 7:60) What? How could he possibly have this type of heart attitude while he was being killed? This ability to offer an intercessory prayer for his very murderers had to be a result of much time spent in prayer by Stephen. Praying was not something he just decided to start doing that day. Rather, Stephen knew the benefits and rewards of prayer.

Think about Peter. While he was imprisoned, the people of God prayed for him. Do you remember what happened? Oh, nothing too impressive. Just the chains fell off his hands, he was guided by an angel, he passed by two sets of guards, watched an iron gate open for him, and he was sent out into the city to continue his ministry! Now I find that to be pretty impressive! So, does intercessory prayer work? I think Peter would say a great big YES!

I have a particular fondness for the words of Paul as he prayed for the people in Philippi. He said, *"I pray that your love may abound still more and more in real knowledge and all discernment, so that you may approve the things that are excellent in order to be sincere and blameless until the day of Christ..."* (Philippians 1:9-10) Have you ever prayed scripture back to God? I recommend you use this scripture on a regular basis. Substitute the name of someone you care about in these verses. I substitute my daughter's name in the appropriate places, and it is a very heartfelt intercession by me for her. God honors this type of prayer.

Even Pharaoh realized the importance of intercessory prayer. He said to Moses, *"I will let you go, that you may sacrifice to the Lord your God in the wilderness; only that you shall not go very far away. Make supplication for me."* The word supplication can be substituted for intercession in this instance. Pharaoh wanted Moses to pray for him.

Undoubtedly, the most perfect example of intercessory prayer is found in the examples of Jesus. He said to Simon, *"Simon, Simon,... I have prayed for you..."* (Luke 22:31-32) I certainly like inserting my name in this scripture. "Carol, Carol, ... I have prayed for you..." The thought of Jesus praying to the Father on my behalf is rather mind boggling. Yet, scripture shows clearly He does just that.

Even at the point of His crucifixion, Jesus cried out to His Father on behalf of those who were crucifying Him. *"Father, forgive them; for they do not know what they are doing."* (Luke 23:34) Jesus was a living intercessor for all His children.

What Do I Ask For?

What if you are so overwhelmed by life, and the situation someone is facing, that you have no idea how to pray for them? That is where The Holy Spirit is at work. Romans 8:26-27 says, *"In the same way the Spirit also helps our weakness; for we do not know how to pray as we should, but the Spirit Himself intercedes for us with groanings too deep for words; and He who searches the hearts knows what the mind of the Spirit is, because He intercedes for the saints according to the will of God."*

I don't know about you, but that scripture holds buckets of comfort. There have been times when the words would not come, but the tears were plenteous. The Holy Spirit took those tears to God, interceded for me, and God honored my heart's cry. I must add this fact. The verse that follows this is my all-time favorite verse that we have already talked about. Just humor me for a minute, and let me recite it for you one more time. *"And we know that God causes all things to work together for good to those who love God, to those who are called according to His purpose."* (Romans 8:28) God knows our hearts and wants what is best for us and those for whom we are praying. That should make you feel wonderful!

Pray For The Government – Pray Hard!

Lastly, we are instructed to pray for our country. It doesn't matter to God if you are democrat, republican, independent, or whatever. He said to pray for your leaders. *"I urge that entreaties and prayers, petitions and thanksgivings, be made on behalf of all men, for kings and all who are in authority, so that we may lead a tranquil and quiet life in all godliness and dignity."* (I Timothy 2:1-2)

I am not the most up-to-date person on political affairs. I do know, however, there are many things about our government and our leaders for which I am not pleased. However, this scripture instructs me to pray for them. There is no exclusion given if we are not happy with our leaders. In actuality, that would be all the more reason to pray diligently for their ability to make godly decisions so that we *"May lead a tranquil and quiet life in all godliness and dignity."*

This chapter would not be complete without a personal story. I have been deliberating on which story to share. I have chosen a story from my childhood. This prayer of intercession was not made by me, instead it was made by my Daddy. In my growing up years, my Daddy was a preacher. He pastored two churches. That would make me a "PK" – Preacher's Kid. Now that should cause some sympathy from you to me. Being a preacher's kid is not an easy way to grow up. However, my faith today found it's beginning in those days as the preacher's kid.

I don't mean to confuse you, but this same Daddy is the one my mother divorced due to abuse. When Daddy left the church, he decided to turn away from everything he knew to be right and true. That was when our lives began to unravel.

When Daddy was following the Lord closely, he had the distinct opportunity to pray with a very sick man. Daddy had been called to his bedside as the family felt death was imminent. Daddy prayed for peace for this man and his family, but he also prayed for divine healing. Daddy left them to wait for their family member's death. About two days later, Daddy heard from the family. The news was not that of death at all.

Daddy was being summoned to come to the house immediately. Upon his arrival, he found this man, who was at death's door just two days earlier, walking around feeling wonderful. He greeted Daddy at the door with a cup of coffee in one hand, and he used the other hand to shake Daddy's hand. He then took his foot and pushed the door shut. These are not the actions of someone who is about to die. This was a miracle of mammoth proportion! It is a miracle that had a lasting effect on my Daddy. Obviously, it is a story that has stuck with me through all these years.

Praying for others is paramount in the building of a strong prayer life. God wants us to share our heart's desires with Him. He wants us to trust Him to bring about the best result in every situation we present to Him. This can be a challenge, for sure. However, it is what brings us closer to God and closer to our fellow man. When we see God at work in lives we have brought before His throne of grace and mercy, we can then begin to pray with thanksgiving. "There is not in the world a kind of life more sweet and delightful than that of a continual conversation with God."

"There is not in the world a kind of life
more sweet and delightful than that of a
continual conversation with God."

(BROTHER LAWRENCE)

CHAPTER FIVE - HOW DO I SAY "THANK YOU"?

T hank you. They are two simple words that can carry huge meaning when spoken from the heart. These words were among the first words we learned as children. We were often instructed by our parents to say "thank you" for the cookie, or gift, or compliment. However, as we began to mature, some of us decided this courtesy was not necessary. Do you remember the teenage years when the "thank you" was replaced with a grunt? Then we entered adulthood, and the saying of "thank you" was often formed on the lips but did not find its origin in the heart. When we come before God with our "thank you" to Him, it should always come from the heart long before it leaves the lips.

Does God really need to be thanked? Is it something that is necessary? After all, isn't it God's job to do for us the things He does? Yes, Yes, and No! Yes, God does need to be thanked. Yes, it is necessary for OUR well-being to thank Him. And, "no", He has no obligation to do anything for us. The absence of an obligation on His part would bring us full circle back to our need to thank Him, as well as its importance to our physical, mental, and spiritual health. Let's look at how saying "thank you" affects us physically, mentally, and spiritually.

Physically

If you are like me, you find yourself busy from the time your eyes open to the minute they close. I often say the reason I don't sit down until late in the day is simple. If I sit down, a switch in my bottom end activates a switch in my eyelids that forces them to close. It is the most amazing sequence of events. This busyness means I was involved in situations where I needed to say "thank you," and if I followed God's bidding for my life, there would be others who needed to say "thank you" to me. I recall experiencing both these situations all within the span of one activity.

I previously worked with the choir at the assisted living where my mother lived. My pianist was a wonderful, caring, and talented volunteer who later became my first employee. She never hesitated to help me, and she always encouraged me. When we finished our hour long practice session, I thanked her for always being so dependable and available to me. It made me feel good to speak these words of truth to her. She kindly responded with the words that made my day.

She explained the time spent working with our choirs is one of the best parts of her week. She looked forward to being around our "old folk friends" and sharing the gift of music with them. It lifted her spirits while she was around them. She thanked me for the opportunity to be a part of our choirs. Our words of thanks to each other filled a need in our hearts to express gratitude, kindness, and love to each other. Plainly said, it just felt good!

The words of Psalm 69:30 are so appropriate for this occasion. *"I will praise the name of God with song and magnify Him with thanksgiving."* I believe our words of thanksgiving to each other are offered as sweet words of thanksgiving to God. God honors our hearts and is magnified through the words being said.

The physical act of saying "thank you" may seem insignificant, but it is one of the most uplifting things we can do for each other. Research has shown there are many health benefits derived from the simple act of saying "thank you." These health benefits include fewer headaches, reduced gastrointestinal problems, decreased chest pain, and decreased muscle aches. In addition, these moments of gratitude reduce stress, which reduces inflammation, and that leads to better brain and gut health.

"Feeling gratitude is a sense of what I would call appreciation, wonder, and thankfulness for what has occurred in our lives and what is going on right now, an eager anticipation of what is to come," says Paula Langguth Ryan of Boulder, Colorado, author of *Giving Thanks, The Art of Tithing.* She goes on to say, "It's being present to the wonders and joys of life as it is, without wanting it to be different, and a sense of fulfillment that comes from within, from seeing the good — or the potential for good — in every situation."

So, if you need to relax and feel better, try sharing your gratitude with someone today. The following passage from <u>The Message</u> is from 2 Corinthians 9:10-15. It is a little lengthy, but stick with me. It is worth the read.

"Carrying out this social relief work involves far more than helping meet the bare needs of poor Christians. It also produces abundant and bountiful thanksgiving to God. This relief offering is a prod to live at your very best, showing your gratitude to God by being openly obedient to the plain meaning of the Message of Christ. You show your gratitude through your generous offerings to your needy brothers

and sisters, and really toward everyone. Meanwhile, moved by the extravagance of God in your lives, they'll respond by praying for you in passionate intercession for whatever you need. Thank God for this gift, His gift. No language can praise it enough!"

Did you get that last part? Our showing of gratitude for the opportunity to help in the lives of people in need will result in their offering heart-felt prayers on our behalf! That is a win-win situation if ever there was one. I just love the last sentence in that passage, so I will repeat it. "No language can praise it enough!"

Mentally

The mental benefits of being grateful are similar to the physical benefits. Have you ever had a day when it seemed the weight of the entire world was resting on your shoulders? You remember those days when every phone call brought a situation that needed attention, every knock on the door was a crisis in action, and every attempt to accomplish something was met with resistance of one sort or the other?

When this happens, I always think my brain feels "heavy." I feel mentally weighed down with the world and all its cares. What is the Biblical response to this type of situation? Praise and thanksgiving are the answers.

There are days when the offering of praise and thanksgiving is one of the most difficult tasks of the day. However, Psalm 34:1-3 states, *"I will bless the Lord at all times; His praise shall continually be in my mouth. My soul will make its boast in the Lord; the humble will hear it and rejoice. O, magnify the Lord with me, and let us exalt His name together."* That is the prescription for those really hard days. We need to offer words of thanksgiving to others and to God. Saying "thank you" will change the entire attitude of your heart, lift your spirit, and alter your mood.

Spiritually

Now we come to the most beneficial of the three effects of prayer. When we approach The Father with a grateful heart, we should begin the conversation with a positive attitude. Think about the times someone has approached you needing your assistance. If first they thanked you for how helpful you were the last time they needed help, how thankful they were and still are for that help, and how they feel confident in your ability to help them again, then you are more open to hearing what their need or request may be at this time. It is not that we are "buttering up" God for what we desire. Instead, it is just a common courtesy to be grateful and appreciative. Why would we not extend this same courtesy to God? There is no one who comes close to caring for us as He does. No one is working in our lives twenty-four hours a day to bring about good as He does. Our thanking Him is just common sense. However, for many people this does not come naturally.

Once again, I want to express how easy it is to talk to God. You do not need to memorize a long prayer of thanksgiving from the Bible – although that is perfectly acceptable and good. You do not need to use any certain verbiage – although there are certain words that can express our heart better than others. You DO, however, need to talk to Him in your own particular way. Tell Him exactly how thankful you are. Tell him in great detail. Remind Him of all the parts of the event, how you saw His hand in at work, and reminisce with Him. God doesn't get bored with our drawn-out thank you conversations. Who would?

Let us also remember to be thankful always. If we are only turned toward thankfulness and gratitude as a result of prayer brought on by a problem, then we are missing hundreds, even thousands, of reasons to be thankful during the rest of life. Every time the car starts, the dishwasher runs properly, the kids come home from school safely, the exams are passed with flying colors, and on and on and on, take the time to say "thank you, God!" You can do this while driving down the road, typing an e-mail, updating the checkbook, or presenting a report to a crowd. The heart can always be thankful.

After you experience this heart of thankfulness, you will experience an overwhelming desire to express this thankfulness, in the form of prayer, at a more opportune time. These little lines of thankfulness sent to God while we are busy with life are like short text messages. They get the point across without a lot of detail.

In that same train of thought, we need to take time to sit down and compose that lengthy e-mail (or prayer) that really expresses all our heart's emotions at that time. Putting the two types of communication together brings joy to our heart, and it also pleases the heart of God.

Listen to the words of Psalm 30:11-12, *"You have turned for me my mourning into dancing; you have loosed my sackcloth and girded me with gladness, that my soul may sing praise to You and not be silent. O Lord my God, I will give thanks to You forever."*

Even in King David's mourning, God brought about dancing. David spoke of his clothes of mourning, known as "sackcloth," being removed and replaced with clothes of gladness, and his soul was able to sing. His soul could not keep silent. He knew he would give thanks forever.

Giving thanks forever is really the point of this chapter. If we think about life, there is never a moment in which we should not be thankful. Even the direst of circumstances have moments of joy. There is always something for which we can be thankful. I know this is easy to write, but it can be hard to live.

I remember a friend being surprised at the joy that still showed in my life during the recovery of my husband from his accident and subsequent closed-head injury. She wanted to know what it was that made me smile. The list of answers was really long. Yes, my husband had a severe head injury. No, he did not remember most of the things I felt were important to our life as a couple and as a family. He was, however, alive. He was getting the medical attention he needed. I still had God on my side, and that had not changed!

When God looked down on me and my family, He did not say, "Oh man, I forgot Carol and Michael were dealing with this tragedy. I better see what I can do to help them." That thought makes me laugh. I know, because scripture teaches me, God knows every detail of every day in the past, in the present, and in the future. Jeremiah 29:11 says, *"'For I know the plans that I have for you' declares the Lord, 'plans for welfare and not for calamity, to give you a future and a hope.'"* Through this tough situation my family was facing, there was nothing to fear. That was reason enough to smile.

Maybe, though, you don't have that relationship with Christ. Maybe you have never stopped to realize His constant goodness. Then let me invite you to stop this minute and pray. Ask Him to come into your heart, forgive your sins, and lead you every minute of every day. As I wrote previous, Romans 10:9 tell us, *"If you confess with your mouth Jesus as Lord, and believe in your heart that God raised Him from the dead, you will be saved."* It is really simple. Now you have the foundation for which you can begin to show constant thankfulness to God. Let's start right now thanking Him for coming into your heart. That is a wonderful gift! So, get started praising! I am pretty sure you are a little behind for the day.

"To gather with God's people in united
adoration of The Father is as necessary
to the Christian life as prayer."

(MARTIN LUTHER)

CHAPTER SIX - WHAT IS A PRAYER OF ADORATION?

N ow that you have read five chapters on prayer, I hope you have been convinced how simple it is to have a deep and meaningful conversation with God. He does not require anything of us before we come into His presence. We are welcomed, invited, even encouraged to seek Him at any point of our day.

There are those who will proclaim you must pray in a specific order. For example, you may be told you should ask for forgiveness of sins before asking God for a special request. Perhaps you have heard you should end all prayers with words of adoration or worship. These instructions for prayer are all viable thoughts. However, they are not necessary. What is necessary is that we talk to God consistently throughout our day. When this action is taken, we will develop our own method or plan of prayer. This will more directly reflect our heart and our personality which will always lead to prayers of adoration and worship.

Praise God Always

Praise God ALWAYS? That is quite a bold statement. Use of the word "always" should make you question thing. Scripture teaches us to *"Rejoice in the Lord always, and again I say REJOICE."* (Philippians 4:4) When we are in regular communion with God, our lives are going to be touched so drastically that God becomes more and more evident in our lives. When we realize this change, we will be brought to a point of praise.

When we are NOT in regular communion with God, we miss the wonderful acts He performs each and every day. Our eyes are closed to His goodness, His love, and His hand at work on our behalf. This being true, the opposite would hold true, also. When our eyes are open, and we are seeking God, we become aware of how He is always leading and guiding us toward the best outcome for every situation in our lives.

If we are constantly seeking His direction, we are opening our hearts and minds, our eyes and ears to the actions He will be taking. We will recognize these actions and be amazed at them. This will bring about rejoicing. This rejoicing will be heartfelt and abundant. It will come from the innermost depths of the heart and will result in an expression of great emotion.

Let us take a moment to remember, however, those seemingly **small** details of daily life that deserve words of praise. Don't hesitate to list them before God with your emotions of praise and worship. "Listing them" may seem rather cold. However, it is my belief that taking the time each day to make a list of what you are thankful for will bring about automatic words of worship and adoration. God will bless both the list and the emotions they evoke.

I like to walk through my home, admire the things I enjoy owning, and thank God for those things. "Lord, I thank you for our home, and I am very thankful for my comfy recliner. I like the new rug under the coffee table and the flower on the coffee table is so pretty. Thank you, Lord."

The Dance Of Joy

Think again about Philippians 4:4, *"Rejoice in the Lord always; again I will say, rejoice!"* That verse leaves no room for interpretation. Rejoice! Rejoice again! Job well done! Rejoicing will please the ears of God, and it will make your day brighter and your body healthier.

There are days in my life when the rejoicing is accompanied by what I affectionately call "the dance of joy." I will be the first to admit this dance is not pretty. However, this dance is heartfelt, and I truly believe it makes God smile. After all, He knows I can't dance, but He is glad to see me try!

Sometimes this rejoicing is accompanied by phone calls to everyone we know in order to share the good news. When we do this, we once again have the opportunity to honor God by letting it be known we believe this wonderful news is a gift from God. That is worshipping God outside the realm of prayer. It is a wonderful way to communicate both to the listener and to God just how much our heart is rejoicing. I Samuel 2:1 has the words of Hannah saying, *"My heart exults in the Lord; My horn is exalted in the Lord"*.

Rejoicing in the Lord is a great way to share the Good News of Jesus. Be on guard, however. Satan is very interested in making sure you do not include phrases like "God has blessed me by....," "This was God working in my life," or "Let me tell you the blessing

I received today." He very much wants you to delete any reference to God, Jesus, blessings, gifts, or anything that might have a spiritual connotation. I doubt he minds if you tell of the good thing that happened, but he really wants you to avoid that whole "Jesus thing." Let us make sure we don't let that happen. Be brave and give the credit where it is due!

Praising is such a terrific time to share emotions of happiness with those we meet. If those words are prefaced with words that honor the Giver of that joy, then we have accomplished several things at once.

One, we have shared our happiness with someone else. Two, we have brightened their day. Three, we have made God smile because we have told of His goodness. Four, if we have included Him in the story, we have shared our faith with another person. And five, we have honored God and had an impact on the listener. You never know whose life may be changed because you gave God the glory for the happiness you were experiencing on that day.

Recently I had some exciting news arrive via email. It came late in the afternoon, and I was so excited that I did that "dance of joy" I mentioned earlier. I received celebrity endorsement for a book I had written! This was HUGE news in my life. I couldn't wait to share this story with those I loved. I thought of calling my husband at work, but I decided I should wait and tell him face to face. This news was too good to convey over the phone. I printed the email telling of my endorsement, and I placed it on the kitchen counter while I worked on dinner. When my husband arrived home, I was busy chopping onions and talking with my mother on the phone. He, so very nonchalantly, picked up the email and read it! I could not believe he had ruined my much awaited announcement and surprise. I was totally frustrated!

I have enjoyed telling friends this story, but the best part is telling how God is working through the book being endorsed. I have seen His hand reach out to people with whom I previously would never have had reason to have conversation. God is amazing, and He uses us in amazing ways to bring Glory to His Son. Don't hesitate to include phrases that honor Him in your story telling. "Because of God's goodness" or "this is such a blessing" or "I am thankful to God for..." are all great starters for most any story.

Full Circle

This brings us to prayers of worship and adoration. It is like the phrase "the gift that keeps on giving." You receive a blessing, you share the news of that blessing, you give God the glory for that blessing, then you go straight back to God and worship and adore Him for that blessing. It is a full circle process. Don't forget to thank God again and again for what He does. I am the sort of person who certainly doesn't mind asking God repeatedly for help with a burden on my heart. It would stand to reason that I would thank Him repeatedly for all my blessings. This type of relationship with God just plain feels good. I totally understand that a Christian's walk with God is not about how we feel. It is about having a relationship with God. However, (big pause for emphasis, please) experiencing emotions before God is a healthy form of worship.

God wants to be included in everything that goes on in our lives. It would stand to reason He would want to hear us be thankful and appreciative for the work He does on our behalf and the blessings He sends our way. It is good and healthy to enjoy the good feelings that result because of this form of communication with God.

Get pen and paper together, and start making your praise list right now. I think you will be surprised when the page fills up and a second sheet of paper is needed!

"To forgive is to set a prisoner free and discover that the prisoner was you."

(LEWIS B. SMEDES)

CHAPTER SEVEN -
SHOULD I PRAY FOR
FORGIVENESS?

Have you ever experienced betrayal? What about extreme disappointment? Unfortunately, most all of us are familiar with the emotions that follow these situations. Hurt, disappointment, sadness, and even grief are very common. Life has a way of catching you off guard, and it is then you are caught face to face with one of these emotions.

I Lost My Best Friend

Some years ago, my very best friend hurt me deeply. She made a comment that hurt me so dramatically I am not sure I have healed completely from the scars left by those words. The friendship was destroyed, and no attempts at reconciliation have been successful. Oh, I have tried many times. Using scripture as my guide, I confronted my friend, sought understanding, and encouraged reconciliation, but none of this was to be. I still hurt and grieve for what was lost.

The question begs to be asked, "What is my scriptural responsibility now?" Matthew 6:14-15 states, *"For if you forgive others for their transgressions, your heavenly Father will also forgive you. But if you do not forgive others, then your Father will not forgive your transgressions."* My responsibility would be to forgive her and move on with life. This is not so easily accomplished, but I have been successful. I do not hold a grudge or any ill will against her. My heart still aches for the friendship I cherished then, and I really doubt I will ever get over those feelings of loss. However, I more desperately want my heavenly Father to forgive me, so forgiving my friend is absolutely necessary.

What If I Can't Forgive?

When we choose not to forgive, who do we really hurt? We may think we are standing firm or making a point because we know we were RIGHT. We decide not to give in or try to make amends in any way. While it may seem as if we have shown the world "who was boss" in the situation, the truth is quite the opposite.

Holding on to situations that should be forgiven is extremely unhealthy physically, mentally, and spiritually. When we keep those feelings inside of us, we actually begin to feel physical ill effects. The holding of a grudge, or emotions that need to be forgiven, can cause stress to build up inside the human body. This stress can be played out in hundreds of different ways. We may see it as physical pain, such as headaches or muscle aches. We may see it as psychological pain in the form of depression. We may experience relational effects as it tears down other relationships in our lives. We most certainly can see its effect on our spiritual life. When we hold on to the pain of disappointment brought on by someone else, and we do not forgive that person, we are driving a wedge between ourselves and God. Scripture teaches us that we must forgive those who offend, abuse, misuse, slander, or hurt us. We are even to consider it a "joy" when these things happen.

Consider it a joy? How could this be possible? That is a great question. Luke 6:22 tell us, *"Blessed are you when men hate you, and ostracize you, and insult you, and scorn your name as evil, for the sake of the Son of Man. Be glad in that day and leap for joy, for behold, your reward is great in heaven. For in the same way their fathers used to treat the prophets."*

In The Lord's Prayer we say, *"Forgive us our transgressions as we forgive those who transgress against us."* If we are asking God to forgive us based on the way we forgive others, then we must be diligent in our efforts to forgive. How are we at doing this? I am afraid we leave a lot to be desired. Let us look at the ultimate example of forgiveness – Jesus Christ.

He Had Forgiveness Figured Out

In scripture we read of Jesus forgiving Nicodemus, and we know He forgave the prostitute when she came to the well to draw water. However, I am most impacted by Jesus' forgiveness of the thief on the cross. This thief said, *"Jesus, remember me when You come in Your Kingdom."*

Jesus replied, *"Truly I say to you, today you shall be with Me in Paradise."* (Luke 23:22-23) Here we have Jesus hanging on a cross, tortured, experiencing evil insults from one thief, and offering forgiveness to the other thief. How did He experience all these emotions at one time? This would truly be an act of God. It would be outside the realm of normal emotion to be so forgiving. Yet, Jesus, as part of The Trinity, was forgiving and loving. Does that let us mere humans off the hook? Not by any stretch of the imagination.

We are taught to ask forgiveness for our sins. Psalm 51:2-4 reads, *"Wash me thoroughly from my iniquity and cleanse me from my sin. For I know my transgressions, and my sin is ever before me. Against You, You only, I have sinned and done what is evil in your sight."*

Recognizing our need for forgiveness, and asking to be washed clean from that sin, is part of the process of maturing in Christ. We then need to take that same forgiveness and show it to those who have hurt us. Psalm 51:10 goes on to say, *"Create in me a clean heart, O God. And renew a steadfast spirit within me...restore to me the joy of Your salvation."*

The presence of sin in our lives, the damage caused by not forgiving others, and the withholding of love to another person all work to decrease our joy in Christ. When we ask for forgiveness from God, give that same forgiveness to others, and, thereby, show them love, our joy can be restored.

Just how many times should we be expected to forgive someone. Oh, my friend, if you don't already *know* this answer, then you probably are not going to *like* this answer. In Matthew chapter 18 we read of Peter asking Jesus how often he needed to forgive a brother who sinned against him. Peter thought seven times seemed like gracious plenty. He must have been surprised when Jesus answered, *"I do not say to you, up to seven times, but up to seventy times seven."* In other words, Jesus was advising Peter to never give up on **anyone.** Just as we are worthy of God's love in HIS eyes, we should consider other's worthy of love in OUR eyes.

Forgiveness is not something we should **consider** doing. Forgiveness is something we are **instructed** to do. It is not an option. Mark 11:25 reads, *"Whenever you stand praying, forgive, if you have anything against anyone, so that your Father who is in heaven will also forgive you your transgressions. But if you do not forgive, neither will your Father who is in heaven forgive your transgressions."*

That is a powerful set of words. If we do not forgive others, God will not forgive us. That should make us pause and ponder. Living with unforgiven sin is like a weight around the neck. It pulls us away from the relationship we need and desire with our Heavenly Father.

Good Versus Bad/Negative Versus Positive

Negative feelings will always crowd out positive feelings. Have you ever noticed this in your life? Things can be going great all day, and then one negative comment or action can destroy the good that happened earlier in the day. These negative feelings can then harm or even destroy our relationships with others. We must not allow these emotions to have control or power over us. We forgive out of obedience to God. It is not part of our human nature to forgive. It is a supernatural work within us.

Forgiveness is not just something we do for the person who hurt us. It is the very thing necessary for us to have close communion with God. We forgive for our own sakes. Either we pay the price for withholding forgiveness, or we embrace the joy, peace, and love offered by God through forgiveness. Forgiving does not mean the person was right, but it does bring us peace.

In addition, we will have healthier relationships, healthier bodies, healthier mental attitudes, and the ability to seek forgiveness from God for all our sins. Forgiveness is a vital part of our prayer life. It must become a vital part of our everyday life. After that, the seeking of forgiveness of our sins will be a natural part of our prayer life.

Seeeking forgiveness of sin is a subject that is not nearly as much fun to write about or read about as prayers of thanksgiving, for example. Yet, prayers seeking forgiveness are vital to a healthy prayer life and relationship with God. If there are unconfessed sins in our lives, they come between us and God. For our prayer life to be as effective as possible, we do not want anything hindering the growth of our relationship with God. Thus, prayers seeking forgiveness must be understood.

For What Do I Seek Forgiveness?

What is sin? Sin is any action or thought that violates a known moral code. In my mind, sin is any action that grieves God. Since my entire moral code is found in the person of God, these two definitions work together quite nicely for me. I believe they are workable in your life also.

If sin is any action that grieves God, it would stand to reason we would not want that sin placing a barrier between us and God. The fantastic news is we have forgiveness available to us. Ephesians 1:7-8 reads, *"In Him we have redemption through His blood, the forgiveness of our trespasses, according to the riches of His grace which He lavished on us."*

I really like those two verses. Look at them again. We have forgiveness. Not just a little bit of forgiveness. No, we have forgiveness based on the "riches of His grace." It doesn't stop there. These riches have been "lavished on us." Lavished! They have been poured out and are covering us. Thus, the forgiveness of our sins is freely given.

No matter the sin, we can seek forgiveness. Scripture does not teach us that we have to pick and choose which sins we bring before God. We are taught to seek forgiveness, period. No matter the sin, God already knows all about it. He knows what it is, why you committed it, how it is hindering you, and where it stands in the confines of your heart. It is up to us to come before Him with humble submission and confess that sin before Him. He is eager to forgive us.

If you have raised children, you can relate to how God must feel about us sometime. Do you remember knowing your child had done something he should not have done? To make things worse, you were sure he was well aware he should not have done this thing. Yet, the child didn't seem to acknowledge this bad behavior. We, as parents, always desire that our children fess up, or come clean, when they are at fault. If only they would be honest, their punishment might be lessened or even forgiven. Sometimes our children are mature enough to admit their fault. Other times we have to force a confession.

We are God's children. Sometimes we come before Him with our hearts in our hands and beg Him for forgiveness. Other times, however, we may need to experience His work in our lives that brings us to the point of confession. Just as we wanted our children to confess in order to bring about a closer union between us and our children, God wants us to confess to bring us closer to Him. In so doing, the bond between Father and child is made stronger.

Why Should I Seek Forgiveness?

Another reason we need to be quick to seek forgiveness can be found in Matthew 4:17. *"From that time Jesus began to preach and say, "Repent, for the kingdom of heaven is at hand."* The very act of repentance shows great respect for God and, therefore, gives Him glory. When we recognize our sin, confess our sin, and turn from our sin, we are acting in accordance with direction given to us in scripture. This pleases the heart of God.

Let us not skip over that part of "turning from our sin." This is found in Acts 3:19, *"Therefore repent and return, so that your sins may be wiped away..."*. Repent and return would mean we seek forgiveness and return to what we know to be right and true. This "returning" would mean we had to turn away from something else. It is this turning away that is necessary for true repentance. This makes repentance a matter of the heart as well as an action that needs to be taken.

The wonderful news is this. Forgiveness is ours for the asking. We do not have to wonder if we deserve to be forgiven. Let me help you with that answer. You do NOT deserve forgiveness. That makes God's gift to us more wonderful. Read with me the following passage from I John 1:9 – 2:2.

"If we confess our sins, He is faithful and righteous to forgive us our sins and to cleanse us from all unrighteousness. If we say that we have not sinned, we make Him a liar and His word is not in us. My little children, I am writing these things to you so that you may not sin. And if anyone sins, we have an Advocate with the Father, Jesus Christ the righteous; and He Himself is the propitiation for our sins; and not for ours only, but also for those of the whole world."

"Preach the gospel. If necessary, use words."

CHAPTER EIGHT - HOW DID JOB STAY RIGHTEOUS?

Job was a righteous man and considered blameless in the sight of God. Yet, his life fell apart. Satan had suggested that Job served God because God protected him and his house and blessed him with possessions. God agreed to place control of all that Job had under Satan's authority and, therefore, allow Satan to challenge Job's integrity. Satan was instructed, however, that he was not to put a hand on Job personally. Satan proceeded to take Job's oxen, donkeys, servants, sheep, camels, sons, daughters, wealth, and his health. He cried out to God through all the trauma, loss, and difficulties he was experiencing. He cursed the day he was born, and he continually poured out all his thoughts and emotions to God.

What Made Job Different?

It was how Job spiritually handled his crisis that set him apart from most of us. In Job 7:11 we read, *"Therefore I will not restrain* my mouth; I will speak in the anguish of my spirit, I will complain in the bitterness of my soul." Job did not feel he needed to hold back the feelings and emotions that were coursing through his soul. He told God exactly how he felt. As I have been told, we must remember that Job had NOT read the end of The Book Of Job. He did not know how his story would end. Yet, he did not turn his back on God. In Job 1:21-22 we read, *"'Naked I came from my mother's womb, and naked I shall return there. The Lord gave and the Lord has taken away. Blessed be the name of the Lord.' Through all this Job did not sin nor did he blame God."*

How could this be possible? I believe the answer lies in the fact we are dealing with a man who daily lived for God. He was in regular communion with God so regularly that God referred to him as *"My servant Job...there is no one like him on the earth, a blameless and upright man, fearing God and turning away from evil."* (Job 1:8)

This relationship with God was forged over many years of seeking God's face and following His ways. Job did not miss an opportunity to spend time with God. Because of this, God knew Job's character was strong enough, and his faith was deep enough, to allow Satan to place this challenge of all challenges in Job's life.

But I'm Angry With God!

Time spent with God is never wasted time. We may feel as if all we have done is cried to God from our grief. Maybe we have yelled at God from our deep pain. Maybe we have questioned God from our confusion or anger. Job shows us that all these communications with God are acceptable and healthy.

75

God doesn't expect us to come to Him only with words of praise or adoration. He is very well aware of the trials of life. He knows the human weaknesses with which we live. He wants to take all these situations and use them to draw us closer to Him. In order to do this, however, we must take all these situations directly to Him. Don't withhold any part of life. Do not fear that we shouldn't be in conversation with God about what upsets us, angers us, disappoints us, frustrates us, etc., etc. God already knows all these things, so it would stand to reason He would like to talk with us about them. He wants to teach us how to handle these emotions in a way that is healthy and honoring to Him.

Well, Job certainly did his share of calling out to God. What Job did NOT do was curse God. Oh, his wife cursed God, for sure. She advised Job to *"Curse God, and die."* (Job 2:9) Job stood strong. As a result, we learn Job was blessed with seven sons and three daughters. These daughters were said to be among the most beautiful in the land. Job said of himself, *"But it is still my consolation, and I rejoice in unsparing pain, that I have not denied the words of the Holy One."* (Job 6:10) What magnificent words to be able to rightly say about oneself. Job came through the traumas of life with a deeper relationship with God.

Satan was not pleased. God was thrilled. Job was blessed.

What can we learn from this? Several points for sure. We know life is hard. We know there will be situations that happen in our lives and in other's lives that are totally unexplainable. Why do children get cancer? Why do natural disasters wipe out huge populations? Why do people suddenly lose employment and, subsequently, lose their wealth? Where is God in all of this? For sure, Job had every right to ask that question. The main point of Job's story, for me, is Job stood strong. He did not know the answers to all his questions. He realized, however, that he did not NEED to know the answers to all his questions. He needed only to lay it all out for God to take and mold and make into something wonderful.

Therein stands the challenge for us all. If you are like me, you want to understand life, compartmentalize, organize, direct, and control. I am willing to bet you have figured out this is not always possible. There are times when we must let go of our need to be boss, and then we must stand under the authority of someone else.

The good news for you and me is the person who is taking that authority is more qualified than anyone. That person is the God of the Universe, and He is excited to take the situations of life and turn them into blessings. That may seem impossible, (you know it had to seem like a huge impossibility to Job) yet God is in the business of "impossible missions," or maybe I should say, "Mission Impossible" like the television show of the late 60's and early 70's. Call it whatever works for you. I call it comforting to know I do not have to solve all the situations of life.

I have enough to do that I am capable and qualified to do. I do not need the added pressure of trying to make something good out of the confusing, disturbing, painful, unexplainable, or frustrating situations in life. Thank you, Lord, for taking all this away and making something beautiful out of the worse of situations.

"Satan does not care how many people read about prayer if only he can keep them from praying."

(PAUL E. BILLHEIMER)

CHAPTER NINE – HOW NOT TO GET A PRAYER ANSWERED

I will admit the title of this chapter may be a bit confusing. However, we have spent eight chapters learning about prayer, God's desire to spend time in conversation with us, and His willingness to answer our prayers. It seems fitting to talk about the things that might hinder our prayer life. As humans, there are many times we may think the lines of communication are down. What causes this to happen? Did God stop paying attention? Did we stop seeking His face?

Who Moved?

There is a song that asks the question, "Who moved?" It says,

"Who moved when the lights grew dim?

Who moved? Are you sure it was Him?

Do you still pray and seek to do the Father's will?

Who moved? The One who promised to care?

Who moved? He said He'd always be there.

You just might be surprised to see who moved."

(Author Unknown)

The answer would certainly show it was NOT God who moved. We stray from what we know to be honest and pure, and yet we expect God to "step up to the plate" each and every time we need Him. In my growing up years, that was referred to as "Spare Tire Religion". I am sure you can relate to how thrilled you were to have a fully inflated spare tire when you realized you had just experienced a flat tire. That spare tire was a gorgeous sight to your eyes. (Of course, it is made more gorgeous when you know how to put that silly tire ON!)

Spare Tire Religion is similar in that we only call on God when life is tough and "flat". Then we realize our need for Him, call on Him, and expect Him to be up and ready for service. While we may lack the knowledge to install that spare tire on our car when a flat occurs, the knowledge of how to have a deep relationship with God is fully explained in scripture. As we have learned thus far in this study, constant communication with The Father is the key. No matter what the subject, The Father wants to be who comes to our mind first.

Where Does God Rank In Your Mind?

I am involved in marketing my business. One of the strategies employed is referred to as "TOMA." That stands for "Top Of Mind Awareness". For instance, when you think of discount stores, Wal-Mart might come to mind. When you think of shoes, a certain brand will first come to your brain. A certain soda will appear as a mental picture when someone mentions colas. That is TOMA. Thus, when we think of prayer, we need to have TOMA with God. Achieving TOMA with God is something that is practiced. It is not achieved overnight. The constant repetition of time spent with God will make TOMA a reality in our lives.

When life is tough, God will be the first source to which we turn. When life is worth celebrating, we will want to invite God to join the celebration. When life is confusing, we will seek His face for answers. While I may have a long way to go in marketing my business effectively, I do realize the importance of TOMA. However, TOMA with God in my spiritual, personal, and relational life is of utmost importance!

Lack of top of mind awareness with God is a way to NOT get a prayer answered. Let's look at James 5:15-18. *"The prayer offered in faith will restore the one who is sick, and the Lord will raise him up, and if he has committed sins, they will be forgiven him....Elijah was a man with a nature like ours, and he prayed earnestly that it would not rain, and it did not rain on the earth for three years and six months. Then he prayed again, and the sky poured rain and the earth produced its fruit."* These were prayers offered by a man who "prayed earnestly," according to scripture. That is the key. In order to have our prayers answered, we must seek God earnestly.

Hold On, My Cell Phone Is Ringing

This seeking of God "earnestly" is hard to do when the phone is ringing, the kids are making demands, the television is on, and a thousand other disturbances are occuring. I wish I could express how important it is to have a time away. Time away from everything and everyone who might disturb your time with God is essential when seeking to hear God's voice. Yes, this is terribly difficult for most of us. However, building this relationship with God will make us better parents, more loving spouses, more effective employees/employers, and so on. There is no facet of life that is not improved as a result of a close relationship with God.

What if you set the alarm to get up just fifteen minutes early? Grabbed a cup of hot tea or coffee, sat on the deck or in your favorite chair, and talked with God? You might be surprised how much calmer you are throughout the day. It seems my life has a special "order" about it that I don't have when I start in a hurried state of mind.

There is a difference between praying and praying with a believing heart. Mark 11:24 reads, *"Therefore I say to you, all things for which you pray and ask, believe that you have received them, and they will be granted you."* I think it is interesting to note a few key words in this verse. It says, "believe that you HAVE received them" in reference to answers to prayers. It takes a deep belief and a practiced faith in God to believe we have the answers to our prayers even while we are making the requests. However, if we are always in communication with God, we will have enough life experiences with Him to be able to pull on past experiences as assurance of His constant working of all things for our good.

What else keeps us from having our prayers answered? Lack of faith accompanied by lack of works could be the key. Again, James speaks of this subject. Let's read James 2:18 – 20. *"But someone may well say, 'You have faith and I have works; show me your faith without the works, and I will show you my faith by my works.' You believe that God is one. You do well; the demons also believe and shudder. But are you willing to recognize, you foolish fellow, that faith without works is useless?"*

There have been many times when I have heard the response, "Well, I need to pray about that." To me that often seems to be a "canned answer," and I seldom believe the person is really going to seek God's wisdom on the subject. Yes, we always need to seek God's plan for each and every situation of life. However, He does expect us to use the knowledge and abilities and talents He has given us to help bring about good in life. We are not to sit back and wait on God to answer if we are not doing our part along the way. I can pray for money for groceries and the house payment, but God expects me to do something to put my faith into action. James 2:26 says, *"For just as the body without the spirit is dead, so also faith without works is dead."* A great way to NOT have a prayer answered is to have a dead faith!

CONCLUSION

Our lives are busy, complicated, and confusing. Our lives are fun, happy, and rewarding. No matter the life situation you may be facing on any day, prayer needs to be an integral part of the day. While we may feel we have situations under control and plans thoroughly thought through, no situation is properly executed nor plan worked through without God's guiding hand. That being true, we can begin to realize our need for regular prayer and communication with this God who wants to be a part of our life.

I hope you are more aware of God today than you were before you started this book. It is not that God wants to "tell you what to do." Instead, He is more concerned that YOU care what HE thinks. I once heard it asked, "Does God care if I buy a new car?" The answer was, "God may not care if you buy a new car. What He does care about is your decision to talk to Him about the possibility of buying a new car." I think that is a great answer. Yes, God has an opinion on whether we should use our funds to purchase a new car. What is at stake in this picture is more than our finances, however. The point to be made is we should care deeply that God is pleased with our decision. This can only be achieved by talking with Him about the decision before we have already made up our mind.

Why would we want to give control of our lives to another authority? I absolutely have no clue. I can tell you, however, why I gave control of my life to God. God is not some "other authority." He is the God of the Universe. He is the King of Kings. Most of all, He is the lover of my soul and My Father. You see, God loves me so deeply that I cannot begin to duplicate His love. With that being said, why would I have trouble trusting my well-being to Him? If all He wants is what is best for me, then I have no worries about the paths in which He will lead me, the experiences that might come my way, or the journeys I must take. God is saying, "Come and sit with me, Carol. I want to hear about your day." I love those times together!

I finish this book with a quote I have heard many times.

> "God is God. God is good. God ALWAYS knows and does what is best for His children."

(SHELTON P. SANFORD, III)

Talk to HIM today!

THANK YOU

To my new friend and neighbor, Faye. I hope you are inspired to pray as many times a day as you want. Pray about EVERYTHING. Pray over those wonderful dogs you train that will later become Service Dogs for folks in need. When you hand these dog babies on to their new owners, let the owners know the dogs are covered in prayer because you prayed for them daily! You were my inspiration to release this book which I originally wrote in 2012. I edited and updated it, and I am excited to make it available to others. Thank you for that inspiration!

A special thank you to another new friend, Tracey, for taking time to edit this book. If something is misspelled or grammatically incorrect, it is all her fault! HAHA!

Lastly, to Pastor Grace, thank you for reminding me of the importance of prayer. In the short time I have sat under your ministry, my life has been changed. I will always be grateful.

ABOUT THE AUTHOR

Carol L. Howell

Carol is a Certified Dementia Practitioner, Amazon #1 Best Selling Author, host of a podcast and video series titled "Let's Talk Dementia," and Executive Director of the non-profit, also called Let's Talk Dementia. Carol loves to share her caregiving experiences while caring for her  mother, Vera, who had Alzheimer's type dementia. Carol travels and speaks to groups about their dementia caregiving journey and how to find joy in the journey. She is a Christian who loves the Lord and resides in Florida.

BOOKS BY THIS AUTHOR

Let's Talk Dementia

LET'S TALK DEMENTIA, by Carol Howell, a Certified Dementia Practitioner and caregiver to her mother, helps to educate the reader on the various forms of dementia. She also provides hands-on tips that make life easier for the caregiver and better for the loved one with dementia. The book is scattered with "smiles" that brighten the day. The author reminds the readers of her motto —"Knowledge brings POWER. Power brings HOPE, and HOPE brings SMILES." She likes to say, "You've just got to laugh!"

Let's Talk Dementia - Take Two

LET'S TALK DEMENTIA – TAKE TWO is a follow-up to the Amazon #1 Best Seller LET'S TALK DEMENTIA. It continues Carol's caregiving story with more information on good caregiving techniques, lifestyle changes to prevent dementia, how to pay for assisted living and memory care, and it culminates with words of encouragement from the podcast titled "Let's Talk Dementia," available on iTunes, Spotify,
and www.letstalkdementia.org.

Momma Is Confused And So Am I

MOMMA IS CONFUSED AND SO AM I is an easy-to-read guide to help readers understand the difference between dementia and Alzheimer's. Author Carol Howell began her journey with the news her mother had dementia. As she started to research dementia, she was surprised to learn it was not the same thing as Alzheimer's. Her journey led her to write, educate, and create a not-for-profit that works with individuals who have dementia and their caregivers.

Reminisce And Worship

REMINISCE AND WORSHIP is a 30-day devotional designed for the individual with dementia. The beautiful color pictures will bring to mind events from the past. The pictures are followed by scripture related to the picture and questions to ponder. The individuals who can no longer read on their own will benefit by having a caregiver read the scriptures aloud and interact with the individual using the questions following the scripture.

If My Body Is A Temple, Why Am I Eating Doughnuts

Have you tried changing your body and found it difficult to accomplish? Have you looked in the mirror only to see an image with which you were unhappy? That is exactly the way I have lived most of my life. This book tells you of the physical miracle I have experienced and the miracle of learning to love myself just like I am at any minute of any day. Then I learned God loves me even more! He loves me with all my cellulite, love handles, and belly. His love is not dependent upon my being a certain size or shape. You are about to begin a nine-week journey filled with personal stories and daily devotions.

Made in the USA
Middletown, DE
01 September 2024

60244114R00056